20 GREAT SON
YOU'VE HEARD ON

FACTOR

&

WISE PUBLICATIONS
part of The Music Sales Group
London / New York / Paris / Sydney / Copenhagen / Berlin / Tokyo / Madrid

Published by
Wise Publications
14-15 Berners Street, London W1T 3LJ, UK.

Exclusive Distributors:
Music Sales Limited
Distribution Centre, Newmarket Road,
Bury St Edmunds, Suffolk IP33 3YB, UK.

Music Sales Pty Limited
20 Resolution Drive, Caringbah,
NSW 2229, Australia.

Order No. AM999372
ISBN 978-1-84938-376-9

Edited by Jenni Wheeler.

www.musicsales.com

Printed in the EU.

Against All Odds (Take A Look At Me Now) Mariah Carey feat. Westlife 6

Angel Sarah McLachlan 12

Angels Robbie Williams 17

…Baby One More Time Britney Spears 30

Beautiful Christina Aguilera 24

(Everything I Do) I Do It For You Bryan Adams 35

Feeling Good Nina Simone 46

Fly Me To The Moon (In Other Words) Frank Sinatra 40

Hallelujah Alexandra Burke 51

Hero Mariah Carey 56

Hopelessly Devoted To You Olivia Newton-John 61

I Believe I Can Fly R. Kelly 66

I Say A Little Prayer Aretha Franklin 78

I Will Always Love You Whitney Houston 71

Nothing Compares 2 U Sinead O'Connor 82

Rule The World Take That 90

(Sittin' On) The Dock Of The Bay Otis Redding 87

Tears In Heaven Eric Clapton 94

You Are Not Alone Michael Jackson 99

You Raise Me Up Westlife 106

AGAINST ALL ODDS
(TAKE A LOOK AT ME NOW)

Words & Music by Phil Collins

on - ly one who real - ly knew me___ at all._____

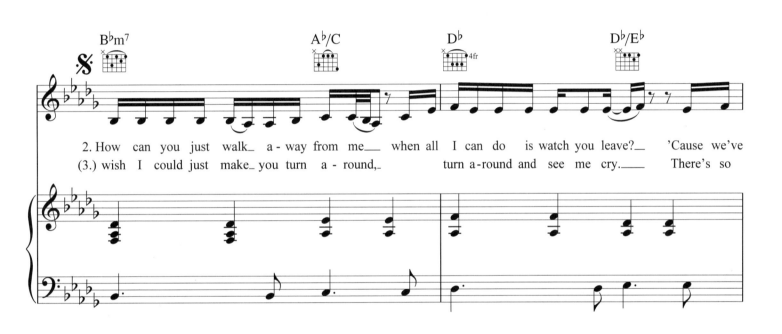

2. How can you just walk___ a - way from me___ when all I can do is watch you leave?___ 'Cause we've
(3.) wish I could just make___ you turn a - round, turn a-round and see me cry._____ There's so

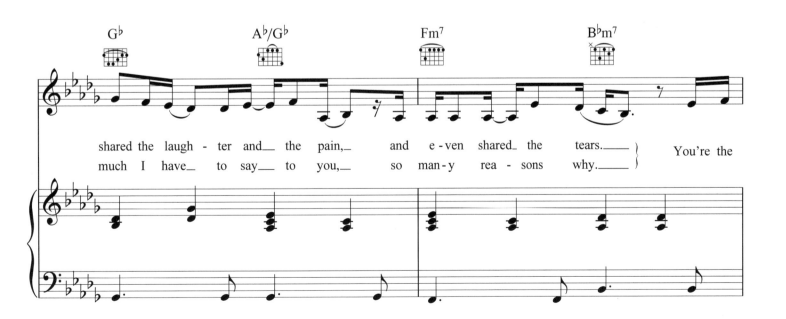

shared the laugh - ter and___ the pain,___ and e - ven shared___ the tears._____ } You're the
much I have___ to say___ to you,___ so man - y rea - sons why._____ }

on - ly one who real - ly knew_ me_ at all._____ So take a look at me now,__

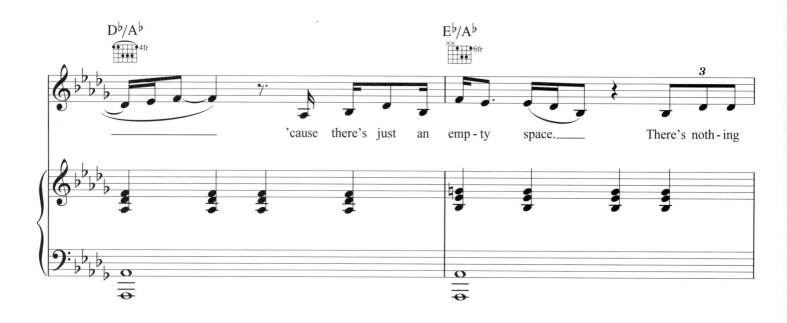

_____ 'cause there's just an emp - ty space._____ There's noth - ing

left_ here_ to re - mind__ me, just the mem - 'ry of_ your face.__ Oh, take a look at me now:__

well, there's just an emp-ty space._____ { And you com-in' back_____

But to wait_____

To Coda ⊕

_____ to me____ is a-gainst the odds;_____ } and that's what____ I've____ got____ to face.____

_____ for you____ is all I____ can do_____

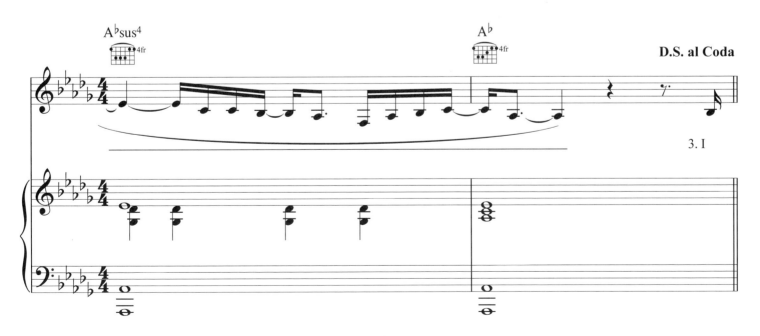

D.S. al Coda

3. I

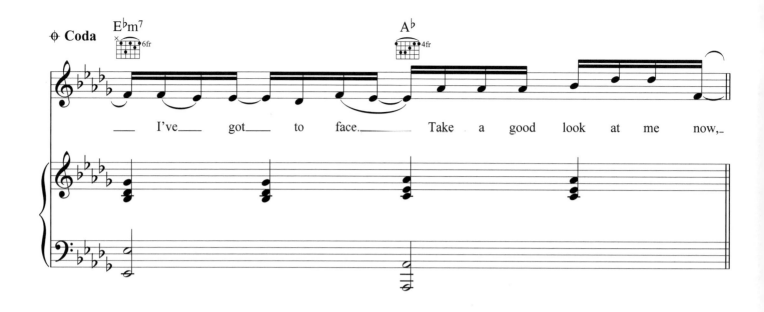

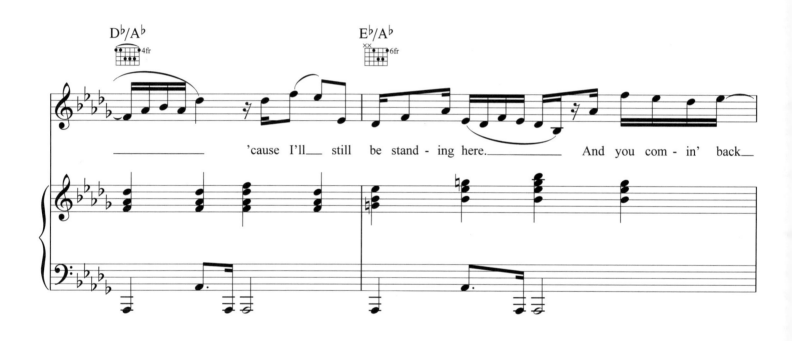

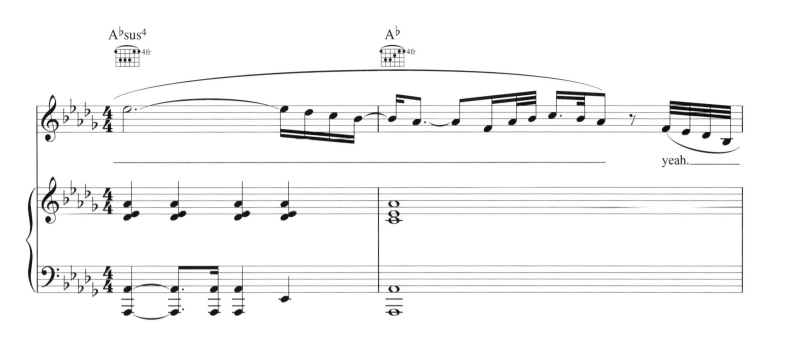

ANGEL

Words & Music by Sarah McLachlan

arms of the an - gel, fly a - way from here,

from this dark, cold ho - tel room and the

end - less - ness that you fear. You are pulled from the

wreck-age of your si - lent rev - er - ie. You're in the

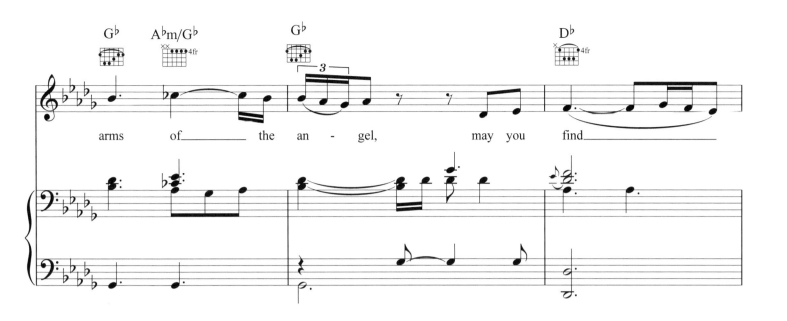

arms of_____ the an - gel, may you find_____

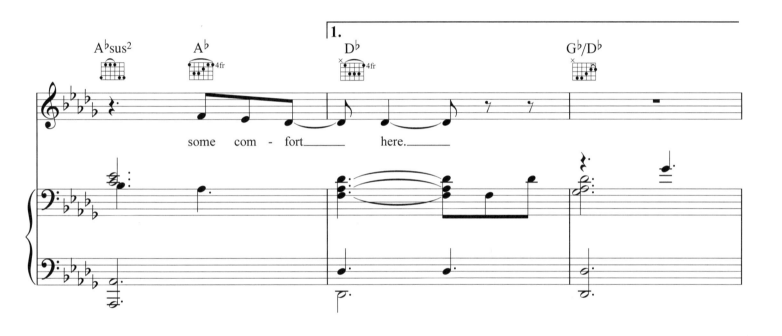

some com - fort_____ here._____

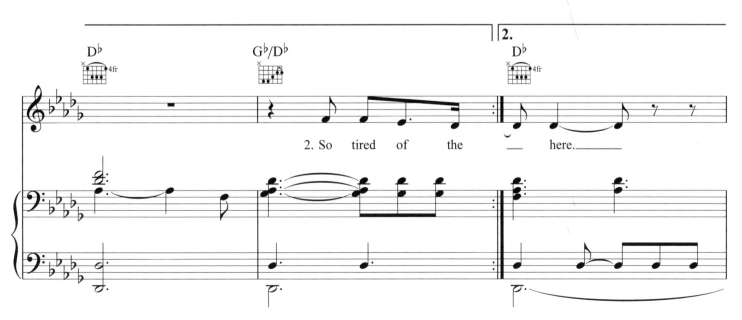

2. So tired of the ___ here._____

15

ANGELS

Words & Music by Robbie Williams & Guy Chambers

'Cause I have been__ told that sal - va - tion lets their wings__

__ un - fold.__ So when I'm ly - ing in my bed thoughts

run - ning through my head and I feel that love is dead,__ I'm lov - ing an - gels in - stead.

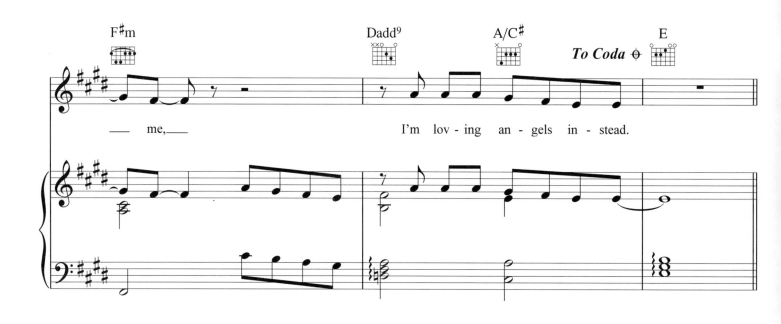

—— me,—— I'm lov-ing an - gels in - stead.

2. When I'm feel-ing weak—— and my pain—— walks down—— a one - way street,

I look a-bove and I know—— I'll al - ways be blessed——

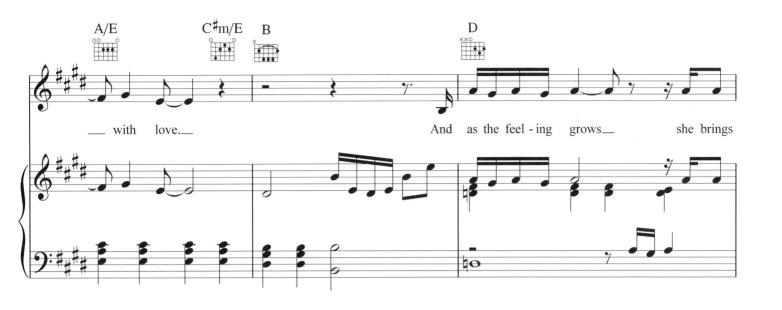

with love. ___ And as the feel-ing grows ___ she brings

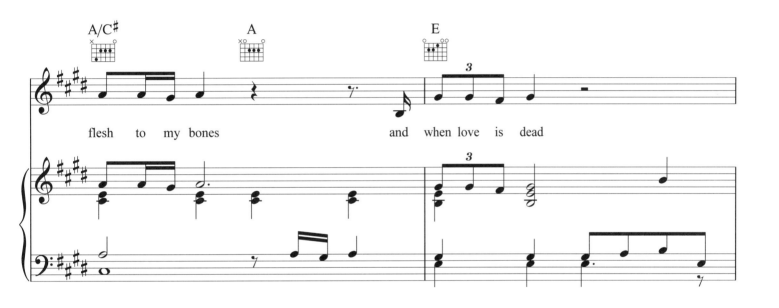

flesh to my bones and when love is dead

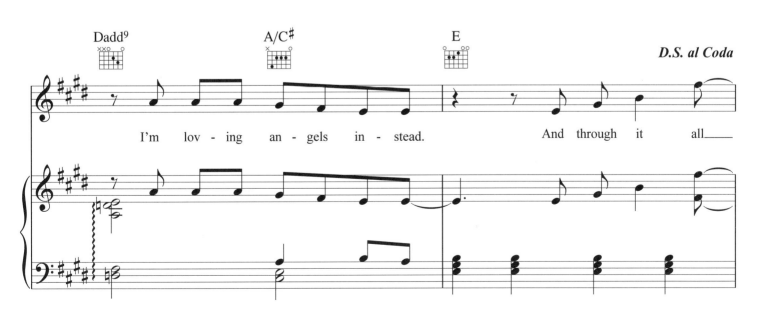

I'm lov-ing an-gels in-stead. And through it all ___

D.S. al Coda

And through it all_____ she of-fers me_ pro-tec - tion,_ a lot of love and af-fec-

BEAUTIFUL

Words & Music by Linda Perry

won - der - ful, then sud - den - ly it's hard to breathe.
-li - ri - ous, so con - sumed in all your doom.

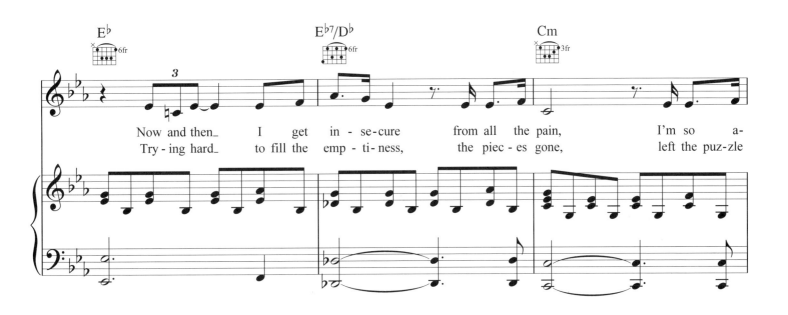

Now and then_ I get in - se - cure from all the pain, I'm so a-
Try - ing hard_ to fill the emp - ti - ness, the piec - es gone, left the puz - zle

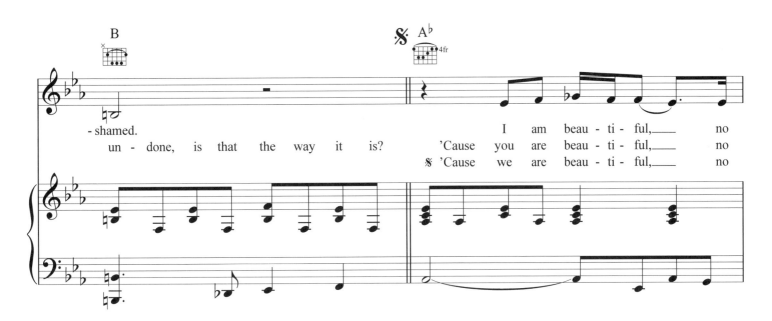

- shamed.
un - done, is that the way it is? 'Cause you are beau - ti - ful,____ no
'Cause we are beau - ti - ful,____ no
I am beau - ti - ful,____ no

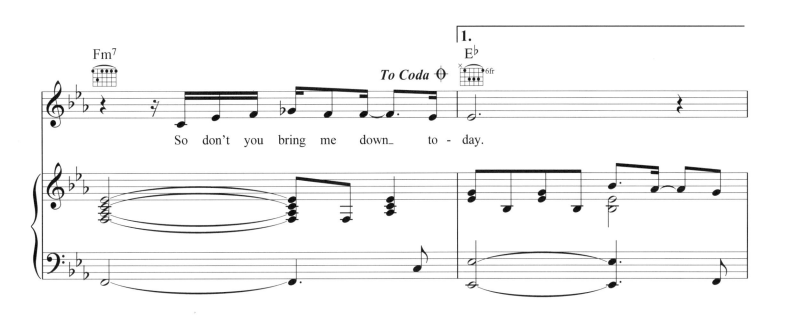

So don't you bring me down_ to - day.

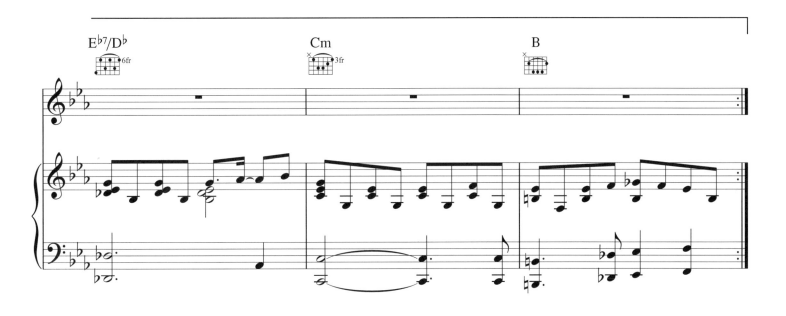

- day. No mat - ter what_ we do,_____ no mat - ter what_ we say,_

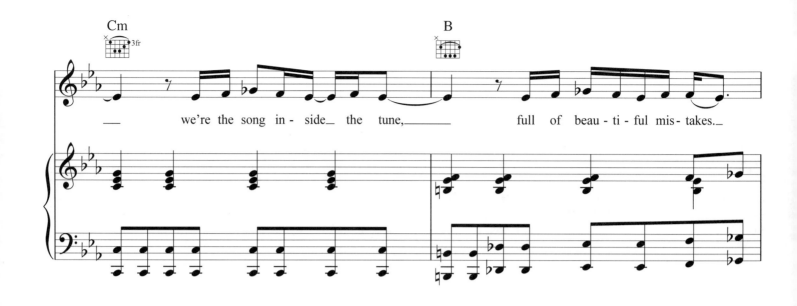

we're the song in - side_ the tune,_____ full of beau - ti - ful mis - takes._

And ev - 'ry - where_ we go,_____ the sun will al - ways shine,_

D.S. al Coda

but to - mor - row we might a - wake,___ on_____ the oth - er side._

...BABY ONE MORE TIME

Words & Music by Max Martin

My lone - li - ness is kill - in' me and I, I must con - fess I

still be - lieve, still be - lieve. When I'm not with you I lose my mind. Give me a sign,

hit me ba - by one more time. hit me ba - by one more time.

(EVERYTHING I DO)
I DO IT FOR YOU

Words by Bryan Adams
Music by Robert John 'Mutt' Lange & Michael Kamen

FLY ME TO THE MOON
(IN OTHER WORDS)

Words & Music by Bart Howard

43

FEELING GOOD

Words & Music by Leslie Bricusse & Anthony Newley

HALLELUJAH

Words & Music by Leonard Cohen

52

55

HERO

Words & Music by Mariah Carey & Walter Afanasieff

Moderately

1. There's a he - ro   if you look in - side_ your heart.   You don't
(2.) long___ road   when you face the world a - lone.   No one

have to be a - fraid   of what you are.___   There's an an -
reach - es out_ a hand   for you to hold._____   You can find_

and you cast your fears a - side and you know you can sur - vive.

So, when you feel like hope is gone look in - side you and be strong

and you'll fin - 'ly see the truth that a he - ro lies in you.

2. It's a

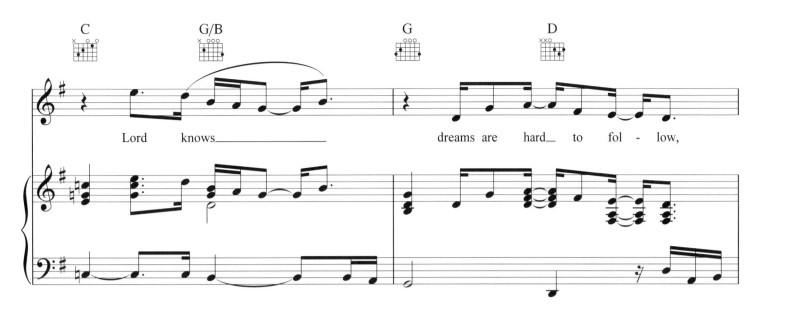

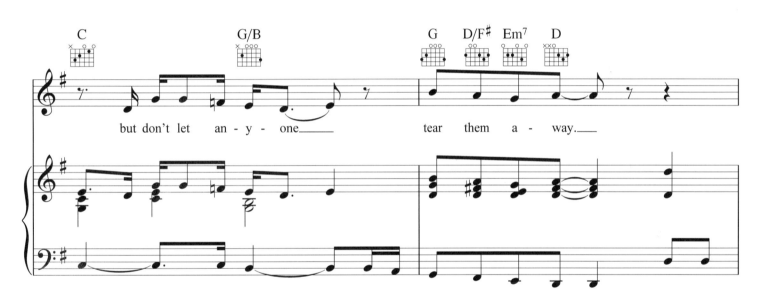

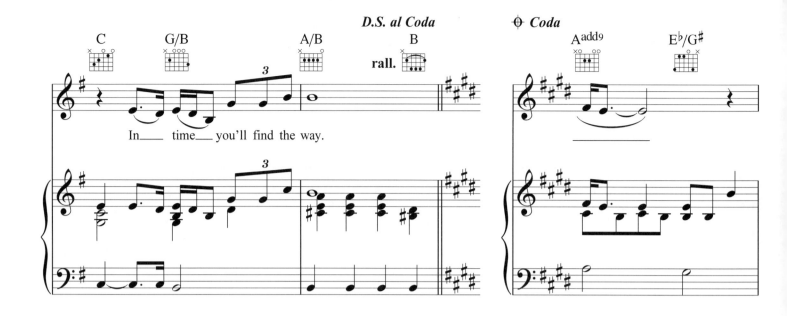

In___ time___ you'll find the way.

That a he - ro lies in you.___

That a he - ro lies in___ you._

HOPELESSLY DEVOTED TO YOU

Words & Music by John Farrar

I BELIEVE I CAN FLY

Words & Music by R. Kelly

1. I used to think that I could not go
(2.) I was on the verge of break-ing

on, and life was noth-ing but an aw-ful song. But
down. Some - times si - lence can seem so loud. There are

night and day;__ spread my wings and fly a - way._____ I be - lieve_ I can

soar; I see me run-ning through that o - pen door._____ I be - lieve_ I can

1.

fly, I be - lieve_ I can fly, I be - lieve_ I can fly._____

2.

2. See, fly, I be - lieve_ I can fly._____

I WILL ALWAYS LOVE YOU

Words & Music by Dolly Parton

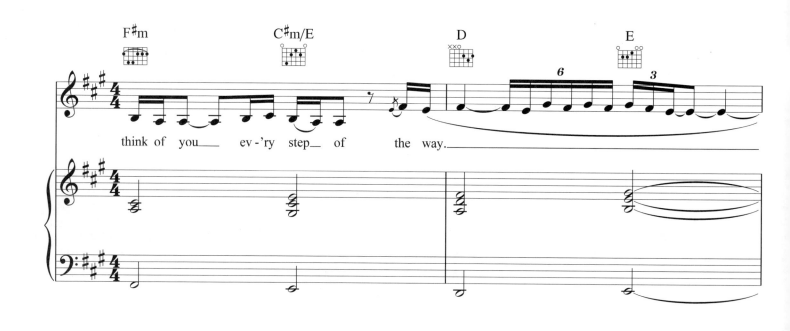

think of you____ ev-'ry step__ of the way._____

a tempo (♩ = 60)

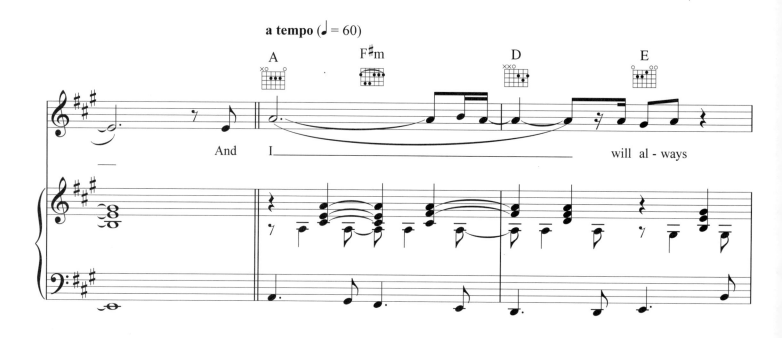

And I_____ will al - ways

love you,_____ I____ will__ al - ways

72

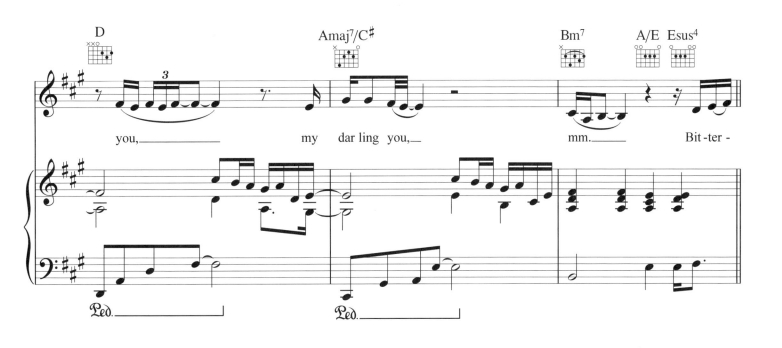

(1st time saxophone solo)

(2.) hope life treats you kind, and I hope you have all you dreamed

of. And I wish you joy and hap-pi - ness: but, a-bove all

— this, I wish you I love.

75

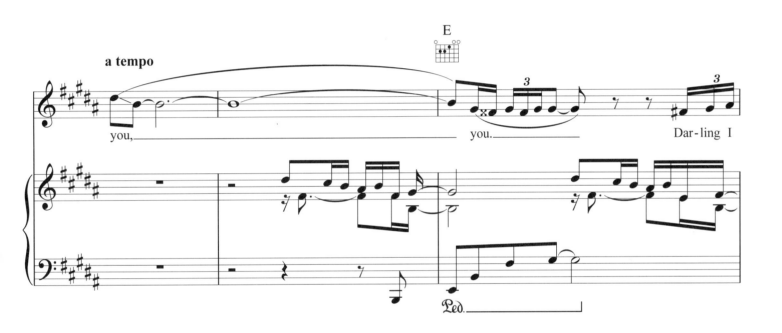

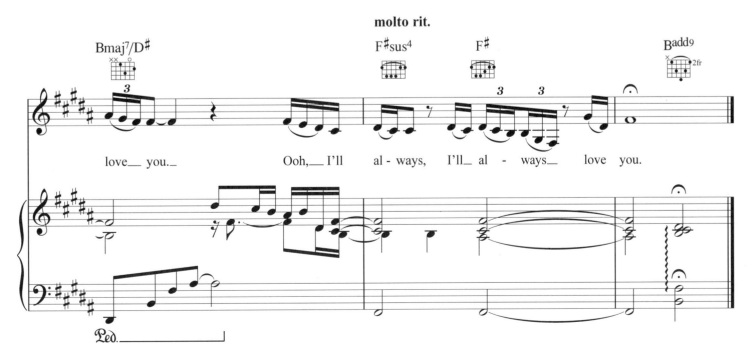

I SAY A LITTLE PRAYER

Words by Hal David
Music by Burt Bacharach

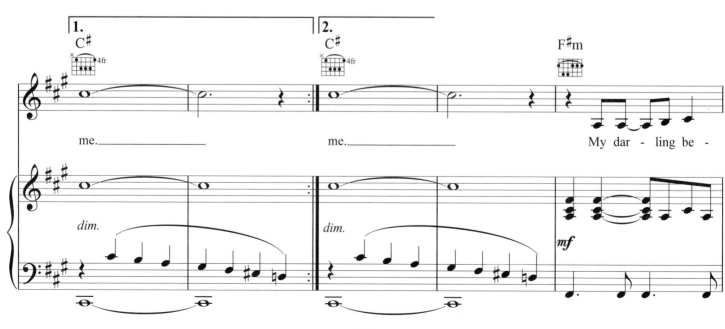

NOTHING COMPARES 2 U

Words & Music by Prince

84

Noth-ing com-pares, noth-ing com-pares 2 U.____

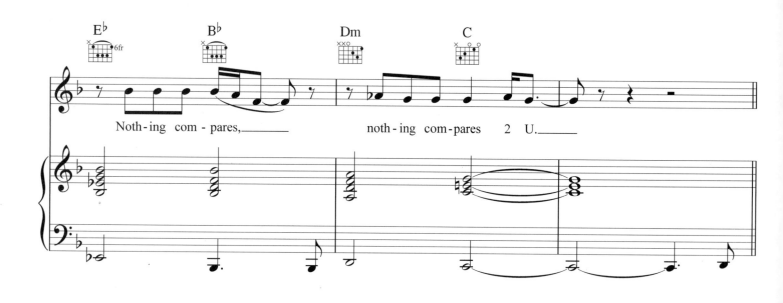

Noth-ing com-pares,____ noth-ing com-pares 2 U.____

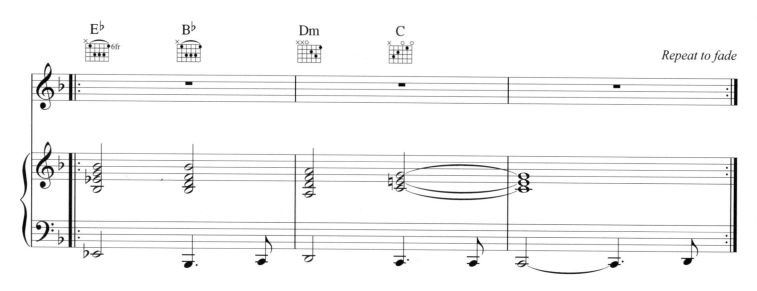

Repeat to fade

(SITTIN' ON)
THE DOCK OF THE BAY

Words & Music by Otis Redding & Steve Cropper

Verse 2:

I left my home in Georgia,
Headed for the Frisco bay.
I have nothin' to live for,
Looks like nothin's gonna come my way.

So, I'm just gonna sit on the dock of the bay etc.

Verse 3:

Sittin' here restin' my bones
And this loneliness won't leave me alone.
Two thousand miles I roam
Just to make this dock my home.

Now, I'm just gonna sit at the dock of the bay etc.

RULE THE WORLD

Words & Music by Mark Owen, Gary Barlow,
Jason Orange & Howard Donald

TEARS IN HEAVEN

Words & Music by Eric Clapton & Will Jennings

Be-yond the door_____ there's peace, I'm sure,_

and I know__ there'll be no more___ tears in heav-

-en.

D.S. al Coda

Coda

-en.

rall.

98

YOU ARE NOT ALONE

Words & Music by R. Kelly

Verse 2

You are not alone
I am here with you
Though you're far away
I am here to stay.
You are not alone
I am here with you
Though we're far apart
You're always in my heart.
But you are not alone.

Verse 3

Just the other night
I thought I heard you cry
Asking me to go
And hold you in my arms.
I can hear your breaths
Your burdens I will bear
But first I need you here
Then forever can begin.

Verse 4

You are not alone
 I am here with you
Though you're far away
I am here to stay.
But you are not alone
I am here with you
Though we're far apart
You're always in my heart.
But you are not alone.

YOU RAISE ME UP

Words & Music by Brendan Graham & Rolf Løvland

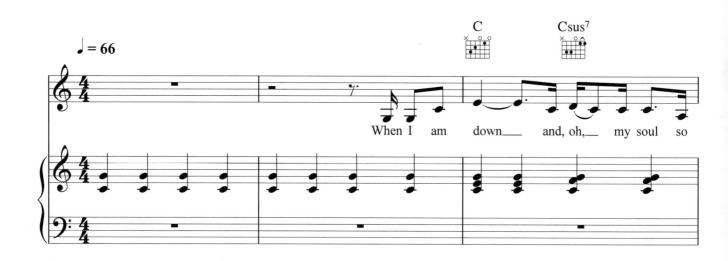

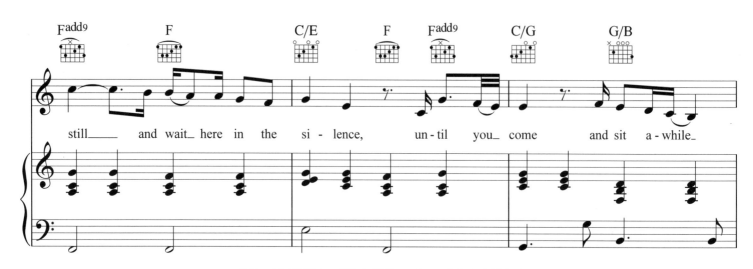

Against All Odds
(Take A Look At Me Now)
(Collins)
Imagem Music.

Angel
(McLachlan)
Sony/ATV Music Publishing (UK) Limited.

Angels
(Williams/Chambers)
Kobalt Music Publishing Limited (50%)/
EMI Virgin Music Limited (50%).

...Baby One More Time
(Martin)
Imagem London Limited.

Beautiful
(Perry)
Sony/ATV Harmony (UK) Limited.

(Everything I Do) I Do It For You
(from Robin Hood, Prince Of Thieves)
(Adams/Lange/Kamen)
Fintage Publishing And Collection (62.5%)/
Universal Music Publishing Limited (37.5%).

Feeling Good
(Bricusse/Newley)
Concord Music Limited.

Fly Me To The Moon (In Other Words)
(Howard)
TRO Essex Music Limited.

Hallelujah
(Cohen)
Sony/ATV Music Publishing (UK) Limited.

Hero
(Carey/ Afanasieff)
Universal/MCA Music Limited (50%)/
Warner/Chappell North America Limited (50%).

Hopelessly Devoted To You
(from Grease)
(Farrar)
Sony/ATV Harmony (UK) Limited.

I Believe I Can Fly
(Kelly)
Imagem Music.

I Say A Little Prayer
(David/ Bacharach)
Universal/MCA Music Limited (50%)/
Warner/Chappell Music Publishing Limited (50%).

I Will Always Love You
(Parton)
Carlin Music Corporation.

Nothing Compares 2 U
(Prince)
Universal Music Publishing Limited.

Rule The World
(Owen/ Barlow/ Orange/Donald)
EMI Music Publishing Limited (50%)/
Sony/ATV Music Publishing (UK) Limited (25%)/
Universal Music Publishing Limited (25%).

(Sittin' On)
The Dock Of The Bay
(Redding/ Cropper)
Universal Music Publishing Limited (75%)/
Warner/Chappell Music Limited (25%).

Tears In Heaven
(Clapton/ Jennings)
E C Music (87.5%) /Blue Sky Rider Songs/
Universal Music Publishing Limited (12.5%).

You Are Not Alone
(Kelly)
Imagem Music.

You Raise Me Up
(Graham/ Løvland)
Universal Music Publishing Ltd (50%)/
Peermusic (UK) Limited (50%).

CD TRACK LISTING

1. Against All Odds (Take A Look At Me Now) (Mariah Carey/Westlife)
2. Angel (Sarah McLachlan)
3. Angels (Robbie Williams)
4. Beautiful (Christina Aguilera)
5. Baby One More Time (Britney Spears)
6. (Everything I Do) I Do It For You (Bryan Adams)
7. Fly Me To The Moon (In Other Words) (Frank Sinatra)
8. Feeling Good (Nina Simone)
9. Hallelujah (Alexandra Burke)
10. Hero (Mariah Carey)
11. Hopelessly Devoted To You (Olivia Newton John)
12. I Believe I Can Fly (R. Kelly)
13. I Will Always Love You (Whitney Houston)
14. I Say A Little Prayer (Aretha Franklin)
15. Nothing Compares 2 U (Sinead O'Connor)
16. (Sittin' On) The Dock Of The Bay (Otis Redding)
17. Rule The World (Take That)
18. Tears In Heaven (Eric Clapton)
19. You Are Not Alone (Michael Jackson)
20. You Raise Me Up (Westlife)

To remove your CD from the plastic sleeve,
lift the small lip to break the perforations.
Replace the disc after use for convenient storage.